CodeWell Academy() and R.M.Z.

present:

Artificial Intelligence in Swift
Made Easy
w/ Essential Swift
Programming

2nd Edition

*Learn to Create your * Problem Solving * Algorithms! TODAY! w/ Algorithms & Data Structures*

Artificial Intelligence Series
INCLUDES BONUS: Easiest Way to Learn Swift

By reading this document, the reader agrees that under no circumstances are we responsible for any losses, direct or indirect, which are incurred as a result of the use of information contained within this document, including, but not limited to, — errors, omissions, or inaccuracies.

Table of Contents

Preface: SWIFT as Artificial Intelligence

=========================== ======

For app developers focusing on iOS or OS X apps, Swift is the programming language that serves as the foundation. Its sheer flexibility and speed highly outweigh the major flaw in the language - it's exclusive to iOS and OS X apps only. Nevertheless, Artificial Intelligence will be a key component in future apps. There will be greater demand for apps that emphasize artificial intelligence - from games to social media apps and productivity tools.

It will always be a worthwhile venture to learn artificial intelligence. As a programmer, it becomes a handy skill set in this ever-evolving world today.

How you'll progress through this book

The most fundamental component of Artificial Intelligence is the Search Algorithm. Its primary purpose is to explore possibilities, given a starting point, to generate a solution for you. We explore the fundamental components of the algorithm, then give you a chance to create it. Afterwards, we discuss its variants, including their strengths, weaknesses, and how to apply them.

A Quick Start

Included is a quick kit to cover Basic Swift Programming. You'll find what you need to get a good start in programming Swift. Then, you'll be prepared to use the many tools and components of AI throughout the book.

========================== ======

Introduction

==== ==== ==== ==== ====

Logic. Rationality. Reasoning. Thought. Analysis. Calculation. Decision-making.

All this is within the mind of a human being, correct? Humanity has been blessed with the ability to think and act so intelligently.

Then came Machine. Humanity has also blessed it the gift of intelligence.

And in today's world, you can see firsthand what an intelligent mind can do for you; carry a conversation, give you directions to a certain location, play a video game as an opponent, and so on.

In essence, only our imaginations will limit us from what's truly possible

An Artificial Intelligence Agent

In terms of Artificial Intelligence, an agent can be anything that, given an environment to focus on, can think intelligently and act independently. It can continue observing and learning through experience. It can calculate and independently decide the best course of action, whether it has perfect knowledge of the situation or just a part of it. It can also take note and adapt to a changing environment.

So you might wonder, how has mankind ever developed something so complex?

Well, it's not as complex as you think.

If you understand the process of how a computer can observe, learn, and expand its knowledge - and how it can take all this information and come up with an ideal solution or decision - then an artificially created mind won't be as complex as you think.

Sometimes, it can take as little as a few lines of code to have a computer come up with solutions for you. Sometimes it can take hundreds. Sometimes, thousands.

Chapter 1: Algorithms: The Essentials

==== ==== ==== ==== ====

In essence, how an AI agent will contemplate, process, rationalize, apply logic, & ultimately generate solutions will mainly be through the use of algorithms.

If you're new to programming, don't be intimidated. An algorithm is essentially a procedure to handle data. As long as you understand how a certain algorithm processes its data, you'll be fine.

Algorithm Traits

First, you'll want your algorithms to satisfy four key factors:

- Completeness

- Optimization

- Time Complexity

- Space Complexity

Now we'll go through each of these and explain them all. Afterwards, you'll explore some algorithm ideas and determine how they fit in to each of these factors.

Completeness

If an algorithm is guaranteed to find at least one existing solution or conclusion within a certain time frame, we can say that an algorithm is complete.

Optimization

If an algorithm finds a solution and guarantees that it is the optimal one, then that algorithm is considered optimal.

Time Complexity

For an algorithm, this is an expression for the longest possible time it will take to complete. In other words, the worst-case scenario when it runs and finds a suitable solution.

Space Complexity

This expression is similar to Time Complexity, but instead it represents the maximum amount of memory the algorithm may use in order to find a solution. This is also considered the worst-case scenario.

Your Ideal Algorithm

After discussing the traits your algorithm can have, you'll get an idea in what to look for when creating an AI algorithm. You want to design yours to find at least one solution (completeness), and the best solution it can create given data it has (optimization) while using up as little computational effort as you can (Time & Space Complexity)

Chapter 2: How to Create a Problem-Solving AI

==== ==== ==== ==== ====

Let's start developing our Search algorithm: an automatic problem solver. We'll have a general overview of it in Pseudocode. Then you'll get to code and run it on your own, with this book's primary programming language.

Abstract Search Algorithm

In its most basic procedure, a search algorithm will have a default condition and a goal condition. It will then evaluate each option it can take, starting from the default condition, step-by-step, until it eventually finds a full set of options to achieve the goal condition.

The General Frontier Search Algorithm:

The Frontier Search algorithm follows the same procedure as above. Given a start node, goal nodes, and an entire network, it will incrementally assess and explore pathways from the start node until it reaches the goal node.

The Frontier is simply a list of paths to be checked. The Frontier Search algorithm will keep adding paths to the Frontier until it either finds a solution or has explored the entire network

For example, this is just like giving a Search Algorithm a map of your local city, your current location, and a restaurant you're about to go to. That search algorithm will give you directions to get there.

The standard data structure to use a Search Algorithm with is a Network of interconnected Nodes. Each node contains an amount of data and a list of connected nodes:

```
// A Node has:
// - its data (any data type you want)
// - a set of connected nodes
class Node
        <some data type>: contents
        Array of Nodes: connected
```

The Frontier Search algorithm also uses Paths: a list of connected Nodes, with the first node as the starting point:

// A Path has:
// - a List of Nodes
class Path
      Array of Paths: contents

And finally, here is a generalized algorithm for Frontier Search:

INPUT:
- a Start Node (can be a class method in OOP)
- a graph network (only requires start node to have a network)
- a goal-checking procedure OR a solution query
OUTPUT:
- a Path from start to Goal (a List of Nodes)
- return FALSE or NULL if no paths found (wherever applicable)
EFFECT:
Frontier Search Algorithm: Returns a set of nodes that lead from the input Node to a solution node if found
PROCEDURE:
- frontier:= {new array of Nodes}
- create a new Path and put the Start node in it
- put the new Path into the frontier

While frontier is not empty {
      - select and remove a Path <s0, s1,....,sk> from frontier;
      If node (sk) is a goal, return selected Path <s0, s1, ...,sk>;

Else:

> *For every connected node of end node sk:*
> > *- Make a copy of the selected Path*
> > *- Add connected node of sk onto*

path copy

> > *- add copied Path <so, s1,....,sk, s>*

to frontier;

}

- indicate 'NO SOLUTION' if frontier empties

Further Search Strategies

This will be covered later on, but how the algorithm picks a Path from the Frontier will determine how the Search Algorithm works.

For now, let's apply the Frontier Search Algorithm.

SWIFT 02a: Fundamental Frontier Search Algorithm

For the procedure below, select an IDE of your choice. If you have a mac computer, XCode will suffice. You may also use online IDE's such as swiftstub.com

========================= ======

Below are the fundamental parts to a Frontier Search algorithm: the major algorithm and its data structures.

First, we start with the Data Structures. We only need to use two essential classes: a network node and a path. A Path contains is what the algorithm uses to store connected, sequenced nodes. It will also be the output type for the algorithm.

```
// A Path has:
// - A List of Nodes
// (can be modified to include more Methods/Fields)
class Path {
    var contents = [Node]()
};
```

Nodes will be the main data structure the Algorithm will operate through; the algorithm will search through the node and its connected nodes for a solution:

```
// A Node has:
// - Some Contents (Data type of your choice)
// - A List of other connected Nodes
// It can:
// - Search all its descendant nodes to find a solution
// (Our Search Algorithm as a Class Method)
class Node {
    var contents: <Choose your data type>
    var children = [Node]()
    // CONSTRUCTOR:
    init(cont: String) {
        self.contents = cont
    }

}
```

Next are two Helper Functions you'll need. This first function helps the algorithm pick a path to check from a list:

```
/*
// HELPER FUNCTION #1:
// INPUT: a List of Paths
// OUTPUT: a Single Path
// EFFECT: based on positioning of your choice:
// - Select & remove a path
// - output that path
// NOTE: you can modify the position assignment to
change the Search Strategy
*/
func pickPath(inout f: [Path]) -> Path {
    let position = 0
    let ret = f[position]
    f.removeAtIndex(position)
    return ret;
};
```

This second function checks if the last node in the path is a solution. One of the function inputs supplies the solution:

```
/*
// HELPER FUNCTION #2:
// INPUTs:
// - a Path
// - Node contents that have a solution
// <same data type as Node's container>
// OUTPUT: boolean
// EFFECT: outputs True if path contains a Goal
// - If path doesnt contain the goal, output False
*/
func hasGoal(s: <same data type as Node Contents>,
p: Path) -> Bool {

    for n in p.contents {
        if n.contents == s {return true}
    }
    return false;
}
```

And finally, the Search Algorithm. The pseudocode is attached to the lines as comments so you can see how the procedure works. The algorithm also uses both helper functions described earlier.

```
/*
    // MAIN ALGORITHM:
    // INPUT:
    // - a goal query
    // <has same data type as node contents>
    // - a Starting Node
    // OUTPUT:
    // - a Path from start to Goal (a List of Nodes)
    // (multiple output types not acceptable in Java;
    // empty Path as output if no solution found)
    // EFFECT:
    // Frontier Search Algorithm: Returns a set of
    // nodes that lead from the input Node to a solution
node if found
    */
    func search(query: <Node Contents data type >, n1:
Node) -> Path {
        // - frontier:= {new array of Nodes}
        var frontier = [Path]()

        // - create a new Path and put the Start node in it
        let p = Path();
        p.contents.append(n1);

        // - put the new Path into the frontier
        frontier.append(p);

    while !frontier.isEmpty {
        // - select and remove a Path <s0, s1,.....,sk> from
frontier;
        // (use helper function pickPath() )
        let pick = pickPath(&frontier);
```

```
        // If a node in the path has the goal, return
selected Path
        if hasGoal(query, p: pick) {
            return pick
            }

        else {
            // For every connected node of end node sk:
            let sk = pick.contents.last

            // - add copied Path <s0, s1,....,sk, s> to frontier;

            for i in sk!.children {
                // 1. Make a copy of the selected Path
                let toAdd = Path()


toAdd.contents.appendContentsOf(pick.contents)
                // - Add connected node of sk onto path copy
                toAdd.contents.append(i)
                // - add copied Path <s0, s1,....,sk, si> to
frontier;
                frontier.append(toAdd)
                }
            }
        }
        // (empty Path as output if no solution found)
        return Path()
    }
```

SWIFT 02b: Using Frontier Search

For the procedure below, select an IDE of your choice. If you have a mac computer, XCode will suffice. You may also use online IDE's such as <u>swiftstub.com</u> or <u>runswiftlang.com</u>

========================= ======

Here, we implement the Frontier Search Algorithm step-by-step onto a simple node network:

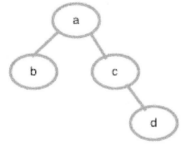

Each circle a, b, c, and d each represent interconnected nodes, which will only have their respective letters as contents.

We ask the algorithm if there is a path to a particular letter from a starting point.

The Search Algorithm would have a letter as an input. It would then check the nodes row-by-row until it either finds a suitable path from the input node to that letter - or notify you that a path couldn't be found.

So we now know what to expect. If we have, say ,'d' as the input, the algorithm is supposed to find it, and output the node path a->c->d. If we have 'g' or some other irrelevant letter as an input, the algorithm will say that it's not found.

Artificial Intelligence will heavily rely on Search Algorithms to come up with solutions and best decisions for its given situations. We will explore more about this later on.

Meanwhile, let's start building our algorithm.

Step 1: Understand & Create the Node Structure

First, we have to build the underlying data structure for our Network. Our Nodes contain the data type we want to use, as well as a list of its connected nodes. Since we're only using letters, our Node data type can be String.

Copy the class code below to your IDE. We'll build on from here.

```
// A Node has:
// - Some Contents (Data type of your choice)
// - A List of other connected Nodes
// It can:
// - Search all its descendant nodes to find a solution
// (Our Search Algorithm as a Class Method)
class Node {

    var contents: String
    var children = [Node]()
    // CONSTRUCTOR:
    init(cont: String) {
        self.contents = cont
    }

}
```

Afterwards, we need the node network.

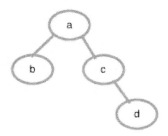

So it looks like 'd' is a connected to 'c', while 'b' and 'c' are connected to 'a'. We'll be re-creating this network in code.

Copy the code below and place it at the bottom of your code file:

```
// Creates & connects nodes a, b, c, d
var a = Node(cont: "a")
var b = Node(cont: "b")
var c = Node(cont: "c")
var d = Node(cont: "d")
a.children.append(b)
a.children.append(c)
b.children.append(d)
```

Next, we need to design the Path.

Step 2: Create the Path Structure

The Path will contain an ordered list of Nodes. Each node will be connected to the ones next to it, while the first node in the Path is the Start node.

Copy the class code below to your IDE, just before where you put the Node class.

```
// A Path has:
// - A List of Nodes
// (can be modified to include more Methods/Fields)
class Path {
    var contents = [Node]()
};
```

Step 3: Start coding the Algorithm

(Before we move forward, it's highly recommended to review the Algorithm procedure in the past few chapters.)

Here, our search algorithm will be a function that takes a starting node as an input.

Since we are checking for letters, the search query will be a String - the same data type for the Node containers.

Place the Main Algorithm below to your Code File:

```
/*
// MAIN ALGORITHM:
// INPUT:
// - a goal query
// <has same data type as node contents>
//  - a Starting Node
// OUTPUT:
// -  a Path from start to Goal (a List of Nodes)
// (multiple output types not acceptable in Java;
// empty Path as output if no solution found)
// EFFECT:
// Frontier Search Algorithm: Returns a set of
// nodes that lead from the input Node to a solution
node if found
*/
func search(query: String, n1: Node) -> Path {
        // - frontier:= {new array of Nodes}
        var frontier = [Path]()

        // - create a new Path and put the Start node in it
        let p = Path();
        p.contents.append(n1);

        // - put the new Path into the frontier
        frontier.append(p);

        while !frontier.isEmpty {
```

```
        // - select and remove a Path <s0, s1,....,sk> from
frontier;
        // (use helper function pickPath() )
        let pick = pickPath(&frontier);

        // If a node in the path has the goal, return
selected Path
        if hasGoal(query, p: pick) {
            return pick
            }

        else {
            // For every connected node of end node sk:
            let sk = pick.contents.last


            // - add copied Path <s0, s1,....,sk, s> to frontier;

            for i in sk!.children {
                // 1. Make a copy of the selected Path
                let toAdd = Path()


toAdd.contents.appendContentsOf(pick.contents)
                // - Add connected node of sk onto path copy
                toAdd.contents.append(i)
                // - add copied Path <s0, s1,....,sk, si> to
frontier;
                frontier.append(toAdd)


            }

        }
```

```
    }
    // (empty Path as output if no solution found)
    return Path()
}
```

It's considered a good programming practice to simplify what a function does. So instead of our algorithm function doing a lot of different things, it will call specialized helper functions to simplify the workload. This also makes it easier for programmers to check, edit, debug, and modify the code.

Step 4: Add the Frontier Path Picker Function

The path picking function for the Frontier Search algorithm is a customizable one in it own right, as modifying this function will affect the search strategy. We'll go over more search strategies later on. For now, just ensure that the function selects, removes, and outputs the path correctly.

In your own code file, place this helper function just above where you placed the Search Algorithm.

```
/*
// HELPER FUNCTION #1:
// INPUT: a List of Paths
// OUTPUT: a Single Path
// EFFECT: based on positioning of your choice:
// - Select & remove a path
// - output that path
// NOTE: you can modify the position assignment to
change the Search Strategy
*/
func pickPath(inout f: [Path]) -> Path {
```

```
    let position = 0
    let ret = f[position]
    f.removeAtIndex(position)
    return ret;
};
```

Step 5: Add the Goal-checking Function

This function helps the algorithm check a path for solutions. It will check all the nodes in a path to see if one of them has the contents the algorithm is looking for.

Since both our node contents and search query are Strings, we'll use that data type as a function input.

Like the other helper function, place this helper function just above where you placed the Search Algorithm.

```
/*       )
// HELPER FUNCTION #2:
// INPUTs:
// - a Path
// - Node contents that have a solution
// <same data type as Node's container>
// OUTPUT: boolean
// EFFECT: outputs True if path contains a Goal
// - If path doesnt contain the goal, output False
*/
func hasGoal(s: String, p: Path) -> Bool {

    for n in p.contents {
        if n.contents == s {return true}
    }
    return false;
}
```

Algorithm Testing

And finally, we test our algorithm. There's at least three major scenarios to think of: searching for the starting node's letter; searching for a letter further down the network; and searching for a letter that's not in the network. For each of these times, we want the algorithm to run through the scenario properly.

Within your Main Class, and just above your main() method, insert this testing method:

```
func printer(p: Path) -> String {
    if p.contents.isEmpty {return "NOTE: No Solution Found";}
    else {
        var s = "Solution Found! Path: ";
        for i in p.contents {
            s += i.contents + ", "
        }
        return s;
    }
}
```

Afterwards, we'll create a few paths generated from our Search Algorithm. Place the code below just after your node network from Step 1. They should be inside the main() method.

```
// test search()
var pa = search("a", n1: a);
var pc = search("c", n1: a);
var pd = search("d", n1: a);
var pg = search("g", n1: a);
```

A search for the starting node's letter should output a Path with just the starting node. So Path 'pa' should have a path with only node 'a' in it. If everything was done right, the code below should print out, "Solution Found! Path: a, ".

```
print(printer(pa))
```

A search for a letter somewhere down the network should output a Path with a sequenced list of Nodes. Paths 'pc' and 'pd' should have nodes 'a, c' and 'a, c, d' respectfully. If the codes below run, then they should print out their respective paths:

```
print(printer(pc))
print(printer(pd))
```

A search for a letter that isn't in the network should output an empty path, according to our current Search algorithm. So 'pg' should be an empty path. If you run the line of code below, it should notify you that a solution isn't found ('g' currently isn't in the network)

```
print(printer(pg))
```

And there we have it. A successfully operating Frontier Search   algorithm.

Chapter 3: Search Strategies

==== ==== ==== ==== ====

As mentioned earlier, the way the search algorithm picks a path from the frontier will determine the overall algorithm search strategy.

Now that we've developed our search algorithm, we can now modify it to suit any situation that arises.

Below are the four main ways that the search algorithm will pick a path to explore. The path picked from the frontier is either:

- the most recently added (Stack)

- the least recently added (Queue)

- the one with the least cost (Priority Queue)

- the one with the most value (Priority Queue)

We'll explore and analyze each strategy and implement them with our search algorithm.

Chapter 3.1: Depth-First Search

==== ==== ==== ==== ====

In Depth-First Search, the algorithm treats the Frontier Options as a Stack. Therefore, if the algorithm has a list of unexplored options it has yet to examine, it will explore the options and sub-options first.

Use Depth-First Search When:

• You expect long path lengths; in other words, the solutions will have long sets of options to get there

• You don't expect any nodes that are subnodes to each other)

• You don't have much space available

Don't use Depth-First Search When:

• The three looks fairly shallow. In other words, there aren't many levels of Option nodes in the tree

• If having the best possible solution is very important

Example: The Depth-First Search Algorithm

Consider the graph below. If all these nodes are placed on a to-do list for the algorithm, the last node added to the frontier would be processed first.

Node #1's options are added to the frontier: #2, #7, and #8. If Node #2 was added last, it would be processed first. So Nodes #3 and #6 would be added. If #3 was added last, then it would be processed first - so that means adding #4 and #5 to the frontier. The node depths are explored first - hence, why it's called DEPTH-FIRST search.

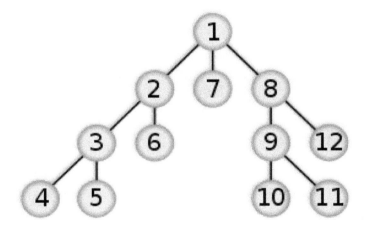

Algorithm Analysis: Depth-First Search

Is it Complete?

Sort of. Why? If there are any loops or cycles in the graph (meaning one of the end nodes link up to the beginning nodes, thus creating a loop) the algorithm might be stuck. It will keep exploring the end node, the beginning node, the path between them, the end node again, and so on and so on - probably in a sort of infinite loop.

On the other hand, if there are no loops or cycles in the node network, this algorithm is complete.

Is it Optimal?

No. If it gives off the first solution it encounters, it may not necessarily be the best one. There may be better solutions that have yet to be encountered before the algorithm gets to it.

What is its Time Complexity?

O(b^m)

Meaning, at the worst-case scenario, the algorithm will explore every node and reach the furthest tree depth. For example, if a node in a tree has up to 2 options and the entire tree can be up to 4 levels deep, the worst-case complexity will be 2x2x2x2 = 16 nodes possibly explored.

What is its Space Complexity?

O(b*m)

Meaning, at the worst-case scenario, a path for unexplored nodes will be stored in memory for every node explored.

The longest path possible is the furthest tree depth. Also, every node has a maximum amount of nodes it can explore.

For example, if a tree will have up to 2 options per node and the tree can be 4 levels deep, then the algorithm will store 2x4 = 8 units of memory

Chapter 3.2: Breadth-First Search

==== ==== ==== ==== ====

While Depth-first search has a Stack for the frontier, Breadth-first search has a Queue. In other words, if the algorithm has a list of options to explore, it will select the earliest added options and sub-options.

Use Breadth-First Search When:

• you don't have to worry about memory space

• you NEED a solution with the least amount of options chosen

• there are some options that can be explored that don't need depth

Don't use Breadth-First Search When:

• solutions tend to need a lot of options chosen (i.e. they're deep into the tree)

• you have a limited amount of space

• There's a high branching factor (nodes with many subnodes/options)

Example: The Breadth-First Search Algorithm

Consider the graph below. If all these nodes are placed on a to-do list for the algorithm, Node #1 would be processed first, then it's sub-nodes #8, #7, #2 would be added to the frontier in that order. Since Node #8 was entered first, it will be processed first. So Nodes #9 and #12 are added to the frontier. Then Node #7 is processed. Then Node #2, which adds Nodes #6 and #3 to the frontier. Then node #12 is processed, and so on. Overall, the algorithm will explore all nodes per level first - hence why it's called BREADTH-FIRST search.

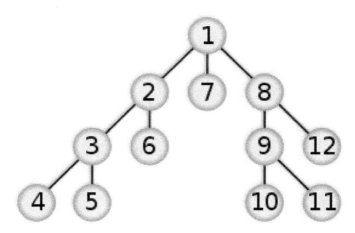

Algorithm Analysis: Breadth-First Search

Is it Complete?

Yes, as long as there's a limited number of subnodes. When there are nodes that are children to each other (for example: Node X is a sub-node to Node Y, and vice-versa), this would normally create a loop for Depth-first search. Node X would be added to the frontier, processed, then Node Y would be added and processed, then Node X is added, and so on - in an infinite loop. This won't happen in BFS. If Node X was added, all other nodes in the frontier would have been processed first.

However, if a tree has infinite subnodes per node, then BFS certainly won't stop. There will be just too many nodes to explore.

Hence, as long as there's a finite number of subnodes per node, you can guarantee that BFS will not loop indefinitely.

Is it Optimal?

Possibly. Because BFS is likely to find the solutions with the least number of options/steps, there is a chance the solution will be optimal.

What is its Time Complexity?

O(b^m)

Just like DFS, BFS will, at the worst-case scenario, explore every node and reach the furthest tree depth. For example, if a node in a tree has up to 3 options and the entire tree can be up to 4 levels deep, the worst-case complexity will be 3x3x3x3 = 81 nodes possibly explored.

What is its Space Complexity?

O(b^m)

At the worst-case scenario, BFS will explore every single node in the tree.

For example, if a tree will have up to 4 options per node and the tree can be 4 levels deep, then the algorithm will store 4^4 = 256 units of memory if it explores every node in that tree.

SWIFT 03: Frontier Search as DFS and BFS

For the procedure below, select an IDE of your choice. You may also use online IDE's such as rextester.com, ideone.com, or codepad.org.

========================= ======

When implementing Frontier Search, the algorithm will actually, by default, either be Depth-First Search or Breadth-First Search. This will depend on one key factor, as we will demonstrate below.

First, let's recall the path picker from earlier:

```
/*
// HELPER FUNCTION #1:
// INPUT: a List of Paths
// OUTPUT: a Single Path
// EFFECT: based on positioning of your choice:
// - Select & remove a path
// - output that path
// NOTE: you can modify the position assignment to
change the Search Strategy
*/
func pickPath(inout f: [Path]) -> Path {
    let position = 0
    let ret = f[position]
    f.removeAtIndex(position)
    return ret;
};
```

Note how the path picker works. The output path, chosen from the input array (the frontier), is based on an index position. That index is set on the first line of the procedure:

let position = 0

When items are entered into an array, they are sent to the end of the array like so:

[0: a][1: b][2: c]   <- inserting [d]

[0: a][1: b][2: c][3: d]

So setting the position to 0 means that the front (earliest) path on the frontier is selected. In other words, the path picker will treat the frontier as a queue. Therefore it will be BFS.

let position = 0

Before path picker call: [0: a][1: b][2: c][3: d]

After path picker call: [0: a][1: b][2: c]   Selected   For Processing: [d]

Otherwise, setting the position to the back (latest) path will need this line instead:

let position = f.count - 1

The line above will set the position to the latest path added to the frontier. In other words, the path picker will treat the frontier as a stack. Therefore, it will be DFS.

let position = f.count - 1

Before path picker call: [0: a][1: b][2: c][3: d]

After path picker call: [0: b][1: c][2: d]   Selected   For Processing: [a]

Now, let's test everything we know so far on the below graph.

Bigger Search Graph:

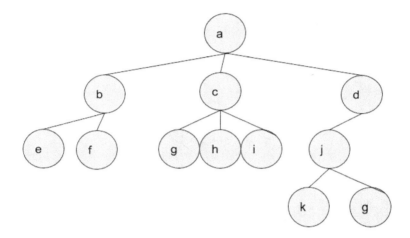

(The code for the graph above is found on ARCHIVE A02)

Place the graph code into the end of your code to create the graph.

We start with the completed Node and Path classes from the previous chapter. If you need to copy the Search Algorithm, Nodes, and Paths, see ARCHIVE A01.

We will then modify the pickPath() method to be either
DFS and BFS.

Step 1:

We'll modify our pickPath() in the code below:

```
/*
// HELPER FUNCTION #1: (Modified)
*/
func pickPath(inout f: [Path]) -> Path {
        // Breadth-First: uncomment line below to use
        //let position = 0
        // Depth-First: uncomment line below to use
    // let position = f.count - 1
    let ret = f[position]
    f.removeAtIndex(position)
    return ret;
};
```

Uncomment either of the lines above to set the position.

Step 2:

Next, we'll run and test the algorithm.

Before we do this, make sure you have the printer() method in your code. You can find this from either SWIFT-02 or ARCHIVE A-01.

Moving on, simply add these two lines just after the code for creating the graph:

```
var pg = search("g", n1: a);
    print(printer(pg))
```

There are two nodes that have "g" as their content. The algorithm will output either one as the solution depending on which search strategy you use.

If you set your pickPath() to DFS, the output lines should be:

Solution Found! Path: a, d, j, g,

Here's what happened after the algorithm processed Node a:

- the algorithm added Nodes b, c, and d into the frontier

- Node d was added most recently; so it'll be processed first

- Its subnode j is added

- Node j is added most recently; it'll be processed first

- Nodes k and g2 are added

- Node g2 is added most recently; it'll be processed first

- Node g2 is a goal. So a path with it and all its ancestor nodes is the solution path.

And if you look at the nodes carefully, you'll notice that the algorithm went "Depth-First":

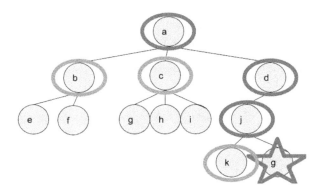

Otherwise, if you set it to BFS, the output lines should be:

Solution Found! Path: a, c, g,

Here's what happens after the algorithm processes Node a:

- the algorithm added Nodes b, c, and d into the frontier

- Node b is added first, so it's processed first

- So Nodes e and f are added to the frontier

- Now the earliest node is c, so it's then processed

- Nodes g1, h, and i are added

- Then Node d is processed, so Node j is added.

- Nodes e, f, and g1 are processed in that order, since they're now the oldest nodes in the frontier

- Node g1 is a goal, so a path including it and its ancestors is the solution path.

And if you look at the nodes carefully, you'll notice that the algorithm went "Breadth-First":

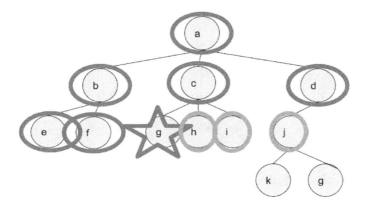

where the green-circled nodes have been processed already and the yellow-circled ones are still in the frontier, awaiting their processing.

Chapter 3.3: Lowest-Cost First Search

==== ==== ==== ==== ====

Sometimes, there can be costs between nodes and subnodes. For example, if a node had three subnodes, one of them would cost 10 to reach and the other two would cost 15.

So if the algorithm finds a solution, the path will have a total sum of all the costs required to reach the solution.

In this case, we want the solution that takes least overall cost to reach.

How it works:

The link between nodes and subnodes are called arcs. They can contain information vital for the algorithm to produce a viable, legal solution. For cost-based search algorithms, arcs will need costs between a node and a subnode.

[Node A] - - - -> arc A-B: cost=10 - - - ->[Node b]

Example: The Lowest-Cost-First Search Algorithm

Take note of the tree below. The red numbers indicate the cost to travel between nodes.

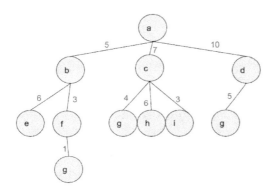

The algorithm will add Nodes B, C, and D to the frontier, as well as their respective costs, 5, 7, and 10. Which node will require the least cost to travel to? Node B. So Node B will be processed first, then Nodes E and F are added to the frontier, along with their respective total costs (Node E: 11 = 5+6, Node F: 8=3+5). Node C will be processed next, because it now has the lowest cost at 7. As you can see, the node that requires the least cost to reach is processed first.

Hence, why the algorithm is called LOWEST-COST FIRST.

Algorithm Analysis: Lowest-Cost-First Search

Is it Complete?

Yes, but there are certain conditions that need to be met. You can't have arc costs be zero or any negative numbers. If this happens, you risk having the algorithm loop and run forever.

So as long as the arc costs have real, non-negative values, you can expect the algorithm to either deliver a solution or tell you that there isn't any.

Is it Optimal?

Yes, and this is the algorithm variant's main strength. You can guarantee that LCFS will give you a solution and a path that took the lowest cost to reach, as long as the arc costs are, again, real and non-negative values.

Otherwise, the path costs will be distorted and the solution produced might not be the optimal one.

What is its Time Complexity?

O(b^m)

At the worst-case, the LCFS algorithm will process all nodes in the tree. For example, if a tree had up to 5 subnodes per node and 4 levels down, you're looking at 625 nodes to explore.

What is its Space Complexity?

O(b^m)

At the worst case, the LCFS algorithm will have every node in the tree stored into memory. So if you have a tree with 3 subnodes per node and 3 levels down, then you may have up to 27 nodes stored into memory.

Chapter 3.4: Heuristic Search

==== ==== ==== ==== ====

Another way to determine how to get the best path is to add heuristics to the arcs. The heuristic values can represent two things:

- A very low estimate of the total cost to reach a solution

- A value to maximize: the solution should have the highest value possible

In the first case, you can estimate the total cost to reach the nearest goal node from the start. It will be admissible as long as the cost isn't overestimated.

In the second case, it will be the opposite of LCFS - each node-to-subnode arc will then have a value and the algorithm will find a solution with the highest value possible.

How it works:

The link between nodes and subnodes are called arcs. They can contain information vital for the algorithm to produce a viable, legal solution. For cost-based search algorithms, arcs will need costs between a node and a subnode.

[Node A] - - - -> arc A-B: cost=10 - - - ->[Node b]
Example: Heuristic Search Algorithm

The tree below is the same one from LCFS, but now with added values to the arcs.

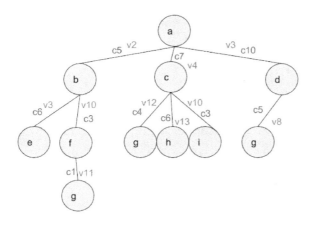

The Heuristic search algorithm will choose its nodes based on either the closest cost to the estimate or a maximum value. First, it adds Nodes b, c, and d to the frontier.

If, say, we estimate that the cost to get to Node g is 7, the algorithm will process Node c first because its cost is 7. So Nodes g, h, and i are added to the frontier, each with respective total costs 11 for g (4+7), 13 for h (6+7) and 10 for i (7+3). So Node b will then be processed next, because its cost (5) is currently closest to 7. Then its subnodes e (11 = 6+5) and f (8=5+3) are added. Node f is then processed, so a second Node g is added to the frontier, with a cost of (9=1+3+5). The recently added Node g has the closes cost to 7, so it's then processed. It is a viable optimal solution, since the other g-nodes have costs of 11 and 15 respectively.

On the other hand, we can also have the algorithm pick a solution that creates the highest value. If we want to pick the path to Node g with the highest value, here's what happens. Node c is processed first, because of its value (4). This adds Nodes g, h, and i with values 12, 13 and 10, respectively. Node h will then be processed next, but with no subnodes to add to the frontier. And once Node g is processed, i would be a viable solution, at a value of 12.

Algorithm Analysis: Heuristic Search

Is it Complete?

No, because there is a chance that the algorithm will be in an infinite loop once it cycles between two high-value nodes or two nodes closest to the estimate.

Is it Optimal?

Unfortunately no, but this is because the value-based or cost-based algorithms can be "greedy" at times. Meaning, the algorithm will only prefer the best possible node it has at the moment, but ignoring all other options. If deeper nodes have higher values, but the algorithm can't get to them because it processes other nodes instead, then the algorithm might produce less optimal solutions instead.

What is its Time & Space Complexity?

$O(b^m)$

At the worst case, a heuristic search will explore every node in a tree and have each node stored in memory.

Chapter 4: Problem-Solving AI

==== ==== ==== ==== ====

An AI agent will have its goals and ideal preferences. Now it just needs to find a way to get to them. It needs to search and create a way to achieve them.

How would it do this? First, it will create a set of options. Then, it will check to see which options will lead to a solution. And based on the goals or preferences we've defined, we could figure out which options will ultimately lead to the best solution. And just to be sure that it works, you can also run test cases for your algorithm as well.

Let's take a look at a self-driving taxi as an example. To get from its current place to its destination (assuming it's driving across the downtown portion of a large city) it will analyze which route is the fastest. For each intersection it will potentially approach, it can proceed or turn left or right depending on the rules of the road. Afterwards, it may reach another intersection, and it will have to choose between proceeding or turning left or right.

Eventually, for each possible path it assesses, it might or might not reach the destination. For the paths that do, your AI agent will use one of them as the route to follow. Problem solved!

[Current Location]
|
|———[Turn Left]—-[Turn Left] ...
| |———-[Turn Right] ... [Reached Dest'n]
| '———-[Proceed] ...
|
|———[Turn Right]—-[Turn Left] ...
| |———-[Turn Right] ... [Reached Dest'n]
| '———-[Proceed] ...
|
| |———-[Turn Right] ...
| '———-[Proceed] ...
'———[Proceed]—-[Turn Left] ...

In the next few pages, we'll try out some procedures and algorithms that generate solutions for you. Each will have different data models and approaches, depending on the goals and preferences you want.

SWIFT 04a: Using AI to Solve Complex Time Scheduling

========================= ======

Imagine 5 of your friends trying to get together and have fun somewhere.

It might sound simple at first, but it can become far more complicated than you think.

What if one of your friends has work at certain times? What if another friend has school? What if he/she has a prior engagement? Soccer practice? Dance classes? Study time? Sure, you can all get together and have fun. However, it has to be at a time when EVERYONE is available.

So, given each friend you have, you need to lay out their time schedules, then cross out times that they're busy. Afterwards, if there is some common available time among all your friends, everyone says they're available, then you and your friends have fun.

Let's have another example.

How do you think a 32-team Sports League will schedule games throughout a year? For all 32 teams, they each need to match up with up to one other team to schedule a game. Each team needs a certain amount of games scheduled in a season of, say, 6 months. There can only be a certain number of games in a single week and there needs to be enough time to travel between cities to have a game.

These are times when a Scheduling Algorithm can help. It will take all members' availabilities and time constraints, then generate a viable solution. For scheduling, it can tell you what times of the day is everyone available. For large-scale implementations, it can be used to schedule sports league match-ups, schedule exams for tens of thousands of college students, and more.

A very simple and easy algorithm to start with is the Generate-and-Test algorithm.

The next chapters will show you the Algorithm and guide you through its procedure...

SWIFT 04b: The Generate-And-Test General Algorithm

For the procedure below, select an IDE of your choice. You may also use online IDE's such as swiftstub.com or runswiftlang.com

========================== ======

This is the generalized algorithm, including the explanatory comments:

```
//INPUT:
//- any number of Lists
//- at least one Goal Function (must return a Boolean)
//- any number of Constraint Functions (each must
return a Boolean)
//      (goals & constraints can also be as function calls
in procedure code)
//OUTPUT: - (optional; select any output type)
//EFFECT: - For all possible combinations of each list,
//check to see if it's the goal combination,
//while checking if it satisfies the constraints.
```

```
func generateAndTest(list1, list2, ... listN, goal1(), ..
goalN(),
cons1(), ... consN() ) {
for a in list1 {
  for b in list2 {
    ...
      for n in listN {
        if goal1(a,b, ..., n)
            && ... goalN(a,b, ..., n)
            && cons1(a,b, ..., n)
            && ... consN(a,b, ..., n) {
          //=== Solution Results are Here
          //Post Code with what you want to do
          //===
              }
          }
      }
      }
  ...
}
```

The next chapters will show you, step-by-step, how to build this algorithm.

SWIFT 04c: The Procedure: Schedule Solvers

For the procedure below, select an IDE of your choice. You may also use online IDE's such as swiftstub.com or runswiftlang.com

========================== ======

Step 1: Your Friends, and their Hours

For each one of your friends, create a Global Variable and set it to an Array. Within the array, set your values from 0 to 23. We'll use integers to represent all 24 hours of a 24-hour clock. For simplicity's sake, we'll only use a single day of the week. If you want, you also have the option to set your integer hours using four digits to include minutes, such as 1330 (1:30 pm) or 1745 (5:45 pm).

For our example, let's say your friends are Anna, Betty, Cara, and Donna. We'll include the integers to represent the 24-hour clock. However, we skip hours 0-8 because, clearly, everyone needs some good sleeping hours.

var Anna = [9, 10, 11,12,13,14,15,16,17,18, 19, 20, 21, 22, 23]

var Betty = [9, 10, 11,12,13,14,15,16,17,18, 19, 20, 21, 22, 23]

var Cara = [9, 10, 11,12,13,14,15,16,17,18, 19, 20, 21, 22, 23]

var Donna = [9, 10, 11,12,13,14,15,16,17,18, 19, 20, 21, 22, 23]

Step 2: The Goal Function

Your goal is to determine which hours are everyone available.

Represent this with a function. There are as many integer inputs as there are friends to schedule. The function outputs True if all the input hours are equal.

```
// Goal 1: Have an hour of the day when EVERYONE is available to meet
// INPUT: Four Integers, representing Hours
// OUTPUT: Boolean
// EFFECT: return True if all input hours are equal
func g1(a: Int, b: Int, c: Int, d: Int)-> Bool{
    return (a == b && b == c && c == d)
}
```

Step 3: Time Constraints

For each of your friends to schedule, create a function to represent which hours are unavailable. A friend's hours aren't available if he/she is preoccupied by something at that time.

```
// Constraint Functions
// INPUT: an Integer, representing a friend's Hour
// OUTPUT: Boolean
// EFFECT: return True if the hour satisfies the time
constraints
```

In our example, we're going to create a bunch of time constraints for each friend. Some have school, work, and other stuff.

```
// Constraint 1: Anna has classes 11am - 1:50pm
func c1(a: Int) -> Bool {
    return (a < 11 || a > 13)
}

// Constraint 2: Betty has classes noon - 3pm,
// then has dance practice until 4pm
func c2(b: Int) -> Bool {
    return (b < 12 || b >= 16)
}
```

```
// Constraint 3: Cara has work 7pm to 11pm
func c3(c: Int) -> Bool {
    return (c < 19 || c > 23)
}

// Constraint 4: Diana has volunteer hours from 6pm to
8pm,
// and work 8pm to 11pm
func c4(d: Int) -> Bool {
    return (d < 18 || d > 22)
}
```

Step 4: The Main Algorithm

We will be using a simple Generate-and-Search Algorithm to solve the Scheduling Problem.

How it works is, for each Hour of Each Friend, the algorithm will check if the combination of hours are valid - based on the Goal and Constraint Functions we made in Step 2 and 3.

To make this Algorithm, create a series of iteration loops within iteration loops, as shown below, for all your friends to schedule.

At the very centre of your procedure, make an IF statement that includes ALL your goal functions and constraints.

If they all return true, you have a solution!

```
// Main Algorithm: Generate and Search
for v in Anna {
  for w in Betty {
    for x in Cara {
      for y in Donna {
        if g1(v, b: w, c: x, d: y)
        && c1(v)
        && c2(w)
        && c3(x)
        && c4(y) {
          // === Solution Results are Here
          print("Anna, Betty, Cara, and Diana can hang out at: "
          , v
          , ":oo")
          //===
        }
      }
    }
  }
}
```

If you use ALL the example code in the steps above and compile/run, here's what it should say:

Anna, Betty, Cara, and Diana can hang out at: 9:00

Anna, Betty, Cara, and Diana can hang out at: 10:00

Anna, Betty, Cara, and Diana can hang out at: 16:00

Anna, Betty, Cara, and Diana can hang out at: 17:00

Computing Effort: Generate-and-Test

This procedure will create a LOT of hour combinations to check. Roughly, it's the number of hours per friend, to the power of how many friends to schedule:

(# of hours) ^ (# of friends)

In our example, we have hours 9 to 23, so that's 15 hours per friend. We have four friends. So that's 15^4 = 50625 possible hour combinations to check. Don't worry; we're just very lucky that a computer can solve this for us.

SWIFT 04d: Schedule Solvers, Faster Version

For the procedure below, select an IDE of your choice. You may also use online IDE's such as swiftstub.com or runswiftlang.com

========================== ======

If you think 50625 combinations is a lot to process, it really is. Sometimes, even for the computer systems themselves.

But what if I told you that there's probably another way?

And what if there's a chance it can solve the schedule with less effort?

In this alternate version, we remove each friend's unavailable hours first, and then we generate a solution.

Steps 1 & 2:

These steps don't change. They follow the same code from the original version.

Step 3: Time Constraints

Here, we've modified the Constraint Functionality.

Notice how they're no longer functions, but direct procedural code to be carried out. Each friend's unavailable hours are pushed into an array, which is used to purge that friend's hours until only the available hours are there.

But you may be thinking, why don't we just delete the item right away? It's because once the number has been deleted, the items in the array after it are shifted over. Once the iteration moves on to the next item, it skips an item.

```
// Constraint Procedures
// Constraint 1: Anna has classes 11am - 1:50pm
var delList = [Int]()
for a in Anna {
    if a >= 11 && a < 14 {
        delList.append(a)
    } }
// (Delete ALL of Anna's unavailable hours)
for z in delList {
    var i = 0
    while i < Anna.count{
        if Anna[i] == z {
            Anna.removeAtIndex(i)
        }
        i++    }    }
```

```
// Constraint 2: Betty has classes noon - 3pm,
// then has dance practice until 4pm
delList = []
for b in Betty {
   if b >= 12 && b < 16 {
     delList.append(b)
   }
}


// (Delete ALL of Betty's unavailable hours)
for z in delList {
     var i = 0
     while i < Betty.count{
       if Betty[i] == z {
        Betty.removeAtIndex(i)
       }          i++      } }

// Constraint 3: Cara has work 7pm to 11pm
delList = []
for c in Cara {
   if c >= 19 && c <= 23 {
     delList.append(c)
   }
}
```

```
// (Delete ALL of Cara's unavailable hours)
for z in delList {
    var i = 0
    while i < Cara.count{
      if Cara[i] == z {
        Cara.removeAtIndex(i)
      }
      i++
    }
}

// Constraint 4: Donna has volunteer hours from 6pm to
8pm,
// and work 8pm to 11pm
delList = []
for d in Donna {
  if d >= 18 && d <= 22 {
    delList.append(d)
  }
}
```

```
// (Delete ALL of Donna's unavailable hours)
for z in delList {
    var i = 0
    while i < Donna.count{
        if Donna[i] == z {
          Donna.removeAtIndex(i)
        }
        i++
    }
}
```

Just to check if it works, these lines print each friend's hours:

```
print("Hours Free (after Unavailable Hours Removed):")
print ("Anna: ");
for a in Anna { print(a," ", terminator: "") }
print (""); print ("Betty: ");
for b in Betty { print(b, " ", terminator: "") }
print (""); print ("Cara: ");
for c in Cara { print(c, " ", terminator: "") }
print (""); print ("Donna: ");
for d in Donna { print(d, " ", terminator: "") }
```

Afterwards, this should be the output:

Hours Free (after Unavailable Hours Removed):

Anna:

9 10 14 15 16 17 18 19 20 21 22 23

Betty:

9 10 11 16 17 18 19 20 21 22 23

Cara:

9 10 11 12 13 14 15 16 17 18

Donna:

9 10 11 12 13 14 15 16 17 23

Step 4: The Main Algorithm

What's different between this alternate algorithm and the original one is the IF statement in the middle.

Since the constraints aren't functions anymore and your friends' hours had their unavailable hours removed, you only need to have the goal function:

```
// Main Algorithm: Generate and Search
for v in Anna {
  for w in Betty {
    for x in Cara {
      for y in Donna {
        if g1(v, b: w, c: x, d: y) {
          // === Solution Results are Here
          print("Anna, Betty, Cara, and Diana can
hang out at: "
            , v
            , ":00")
          //===
        }
      }
    }
  }
}
```

If you run the code overall, they'll generate the same hours available: 9 & 10 am; and 4 & 5 pm (16:00 and 17:00, respectively).

Computing Effort: Generate-and-Test

The original list had 50625 hour combinations to check.

In this alternate version - after all unavailable hours were removed - we have a total of 12 x 11 x 10 x 10 = 13200 versions to check.

The Constraint procedures didn't take much effort either. Each friend's array of hours were only iterated through at least twice; once to check for unavailable hours, and twice or more to remove them.

Between both versions, the difference was tens of thousands of combinations.

If it doesn't seem like much now, if this procedure were to check HUNDREDS or THOUSANDS of people - and their available hours - then different versions of the procedure can have HUGE differences in their efforts spent.

So always remember: when you design algorithms of any sort, you have to take the procedure times and memory space into account. If there's a more efficient procedure, use it.

Chapter 5: Logic & Reasoning

==== ==== ==== ==== ====

Logic and AI?

Boolean, or "True/False" logic is widely used in the field of Artificial Intelligence. It is essentially working with a collection of facts and statements that are either true or false.

Think of the implementations for AI. You can use logic-based programming to have an AI agent make better decisions based on certain conditions. Further, you can have an AI agent diagnose technical problems, and even have AI agents take actions for you - such as fetch coffee (if the robot meets certain conditions, that is).

Why use Logic?

Perhaps the most compelling reason is how simple, easy, and natural it is to express facts and statements as true or false. You can have a statement such as "We're having steak dinner tonight", yet it clearly can't be represented by numbers. You can also try assigning variables as strings or objects as such, but that will require more time and effort.

But as a boolean, the statement "We're having steak dinner tonight" will either be True or False. It's that simple; either it's true (we really are having steak dinner tonight) or it's false.

An AI agent can use several true/false statements and combine them in complex ways. And even so, the AI agent will manage the information much more easily. This is because one true statement can lead to another, then another, resulting in a conclusion, decision, or even a course of action for the agent.

Adding more Logic

We can even add more facts and knowledge easily, if needed. There can be one true fact or two. Then two true or false facts lead to another truth. Then another. For example, we can say a true statement such as, "it's sunny outside", then another such as "it's warm outside". These statements can lead to another truth: "It's sunny AND warm outside. Therefore, I will be running for a mile".

If you put the above together into a proposition statement, it would look like so:

"I will be running for a mile" <— "it's sunny outside" AND "it's sunny outside"

And if you use variable labels to represent the above statements, it would look like so:

c <— b AND a

Debugging with Logic

Conversely, you can use logic to explain the root causes of a certain fact. If one statement is true, it can be explained and justified by another fact, then those facts are justified by more facts, and so on. Here's an example: you realize that "the remote control is not turning on the TV." You carefully look at the remote and realize "its batteries are dead". You change the batteries on the remote, try to turn on the TV, and realize that it's still not turning on. You check the TV power cord and realize "it's not plugged in." Okay, you plug it in, try to turn it on again. And this time, it works.

You can have the above as step-by-step logic statements as so:

1) True: "The remote control is NOT turning on the TV."

2) True: "TV power cord is NOT plugged in"

3) True: "Remote batteries are NOT charged"

AND "TV power cord is NOT plugged in"

This procedure is often used for debugging; if you find something that doesn't work, you must go back and examine the inner workings to figure out what's causing it.

How AI analyzes a Logic-Based System

An AI agent can analyze a given system based on whether or not certain conditions are true. Those conditions will lead to other conditions being true or not, then other conditions, and so on.

There are two general procedures to do this. First is a top-down diagnosis, where the procedure will check certain key conditions (most likely topmost statements that affect other conditions), then go through the system to see what results.

The other is a bottom-up diagnosis, where the procedure will check why a certain end condition is or isn't what it should be. This is done by checking what other conditions lead it to be the way it is.

SWIFT 05a: Using Logic-Based AI

For the procedure below, select an IDE of your choice. You may also use online IDE's such as swiftstub.com or runswiftlang.com

==

There are plenty of designs and systems out there. Almost all of them can be represented as logic-based systems - which can be managed by AI systems to diagnose, repair, and analyze. However, in order to have the AI agent manage the system well, its programmer must understand the system very well. The programmer then has to represent the system as a logical code very well.

For example, the electric wiring system in your house can be built using a series of true/false systems. The plugs in the wall, as well as the lights in your room, are all true/false switches that receive their feed from circuit breakers and wiring panels - more sets of true/false switches. This design benefits home developers, as they can trace the main power coming from outside and figure out whether or not electrical power flows to all plugs, lights, and generally anything that needs electricity in the house.

This design also benefits house residents; if a certain light or plug isn't working, the wiring can be traced all the way to the outside source to see where is the electricity getting cut off.

Water Flow In a House Example:

Below is a diagram for water flow for a 1-bedroom suite:

There are taps for the bath tub, washroom sink, and kitchen. The laundry washer can activate for a short time, using some combination of hot and cold water. The toilet has a switch that directs flow to it. The toilet is either flushing or not. Also, there is a switch that either feeds water onto the boiler system or not. There are also taps labelled A to H that stop or allow water flow. And lastly, the Main Water Switch either allows or stops overall water flow into the suite.

Whether or not water will flow from a certain water source will depend on the connections, taps, and switches in the house.

Where are the Switches & Taps?

The first thing you'll want to do is identify which points of water flow in the system above can be toggled on and off.

If you look at the diagram, the switches:

- the pair of hot/cold taps for the bathtub, washroom, and kitchen

- A pair of hot/cold switches laundry washer

- taps labelled A - H

- The Boiler Switch

- The Main Water Switch

These will be boolean taps that are either TRUE, FALSE, or dependent on the true/false state of another switch/tap.

Representing the System as Logical Statements

At this stage, it's best not to code yet. We need to determine how each of the switches feeds water to the next switch - all the way to the end taps that give water to the residents.

We can start with the toilet. House residents use the water by flushing the toilet. We can have a statement such as, "The Toilet can Flush. Therefore, it is connected to the water supply" ; The logic notation is shown below:

// ToiletFlushable <- ToiletConnected

We can see that taps A, B, C, and D affect its water flow, as well as the Toilet Connector and the Main Water Switch:

// ToiletConnected <- D and C
// C <- B and A
// A <- MainWaterSwitch

Now we can move on to the rest of the house. For one, both the Kitchen Taps and the Laundry washer depend on taps E and C, which depend on taps B, A, and ultimately, the Main Water Switch. Since both the Kitchen and Laundry use hot water, both of them also depend on tap H.

// KitchenTap_Hot <- H
// KitchenTap_Cold <- E and C
// LaundryWasher_Hot <- H
// LaundryWasher_Cold <- E and C
// F and H <- BoilerSwitch

The Washroom and Bathtub taps each have a hot and cold tap. The washroom cold tap depends on switch C while the hot tap depends on taps F and G.

```
// WashroomTap_Hot <- F and G
// WashroomTap_Cold <- C
```

And lastly, the bathtub cold water tap depends on tap B releasing water, while the hot water tap depends on tap F to release water.

```
// BathTubTap_Hot <- F
// BathTubTap_Cold <- B
```

If you have everything together, it will look like this:

```
// ToiletFlushable <- ToiletConnected
// ToiletConnected <- D and C
// C <- B
// B <- A
// A <- MainWaterSwitch
// KitchenTap_Hot <- H
// KitchenTap_Cold <- E and C
// LaundryWasher_Hot <- H
// LaundryWasher_Cold <- E and C
```

```
// BathTubTap_Hot <- F
// BathTubTap_Cold <- B
// WashroomTap_Hot <- F and G
// WashroomTap_Cold <- C
// F and H <- BoilerSwitch
```

Using AI to Analyze a system

Because we've mapped out the logical links between facts (namely, we now know which taps and switches feed water into what) we can start creating procedure to analyze and diagnose the system.

We'll create both top-down and bottom-up diagnoses for this system, explaining what happens for each one.

The Top-Down Procedure:

Based on how the system was mapped out using boolean logic, we've found five root taps and switches that affect the rest of the water system - the Main Water Switch, the Boiler Switch, and taps D, E, and G. Therefore, a Top-down procedure can determine which water sources within the house are affected.

You can find the Procedure Code in the Archive section

The Bottom-Up Procedure:

Here, the same five root taps and switches are global variables you can toggle true/false. Then you can run the procedure for one of the water sources in the house to check whether or not water flows through it.

You can also find the Procedure Code in the Archive section

Chapter 6: Environment Representation for AI

==== ==== ==== ==== ====

Representation Scheme

For an Artificial Intelligence unit to be able to generate data and solutions for you, it will usually need some sort of data source.

And sometimes, this data source depends on the environment: the AI agent will need to determine and observe the environment that it's focused on.

Therefore, the AI agent will need to represent its environment in data. Afterwards, it can process that data with its own algorithms and generate solutions.

SWIFT 06a: Environment Models with Swift

For the procedure below, select an IDE of your choice. You may also use online IDE's such as swiftstub.com or runswiftlang.com

=========================== ======

Modelling the Environment

A very crucial element in artificial intelligence is having a code model of its focused environment. For your AI agent to be able to create solutions, it needs to know about its environment and surroundings.

So to model the AI agent's environment, there are two main ways to do so.

First, you can either use the "Traffic Light" principle - have enumerations of the possible states or conditions of the AI agent's focus. This is a very simple representation of an environment.

For example, an AI agent can monitor the traffic lights in your closest intersection and determine which colour the light will be (either Red, Yellow, or Green).

Use this for making very simple interpretations of whatever the AI agent focuses on.

```
var trafficLights = ["Red", "Yellow", "Green"]
```

Second, you can describe the environment features into detailed data representations. With Object-Oriented Programming, you can simply create class objects about your AI's environment observations - including the many little details as class fields. Use this for more natural, detailed environment observations.

```
class BeachVisit {
    var location: String
    var timeDate: Int
    var tide: String
    var crowdSize: String
    var temperature: String
```

```
init(loc: String,
     t: Int,
     tide: String,
     crowd: String,
     temp: String) {
  self.location = loc
  self.timeDate = t
  self.tide = tide
  self.crowdSize = crowd
  self.temperature = temp
  }
}

var b1 = BeachVisit(loc: "Santa Monica Beach",
  t: 0845,
  tide: "high",
  crowd: "large",
  temp: "81f")

var b2 = BeachVisit(loc: "Santa Monica Beach",
  t: 1123,
  tide: "medium",
  crowd: "medium",
  temp: "78f")
```

Environment Models using Data Combinations

If you choose your AI agent to describe environments via Object-Oriented Programming, you can also link two objects from different classes. You create a relationship between them, taking note of how they are linked together.

For example, we can take our beach visit objects and link them together with photos:

```
// (assume instances b1 - b25 have been created)
// all beach visits into an array:
var allBeachVisits = [b1, b2, b3, b4, b5]

// (assume instances ph1 - ph7 have been created)
// all photos into an array:
var allPhotos = [ph1, ph2, ph3, ph4, ph5, ph6, ph7]

// Possible Relation Propositions:
// #1: PhotosTaken
// proposition: return TRUE if photo has been taken
during  Beach Visit
photoTakenAtVisit(photo: ph1, beachVisit: b3)
```

// #2: PhotosTaken
// proposition: return TRUE if photo has been taken at Beach Visit location
photoTakenHere(photo: ph3, beachVisit: b5)

SWIFT 06b: Creating a Model Environment

For the procedure below, select an IDE of your choice. You may also use online IDE's such as swiftstub.com or runswiftlang.com

============================ ======

Now let's practice creating environments for our AI to examine. This will all come together later on, as an AI agent will have a chance to explore its environment with its given knowledge and abilities.

Modelling A House

The most simple way you can model an environment is the Traffic Light principle mentioned earlier.

If you model your house in a simple enumeration-type data collection, you might have something similar below:

```
var myHouse = ["livingRoom", "diningRoom", "den",
"bathroom1", "bathroom2", "hallway", "bedroom1",
"bedroom2", "patio"]
```

You may also model your house using Object-Oriented Programming. You can represent every room in the house as a Room object.

```
// A Room has:
// - a name
// - adjacent, connected rooms
class Room {
    var name: String
    var connected = [Room]()

    init(n: String) {
        self.name = n
    }

    func add(r: Room) {
        self.connected.append(r)
    }
}
```

To keep things very simple for now, you can model a simple condo in the heart of a thriving downtown core.

```
// Create 5 rooms in a simple condo in the City
var kitchen = Room(n: "kitchen")
var livRM = Room(n: "livingRoom")
var dineRM = Room(n: "diningRoom")
var bd = Room(n: "bedroom")
var wr = Room(n: "washroom")

/*
// Connect all rooms as so:
// <-> Washroom <-> Bedroom <-> livingRoom <->
Kitchen <-> DiningRoom <->
*/

kitchen.connected += [livRM, dineRM]
livRM.connected += [bd, kitchen]
bd.connected += [wr, livRM]
wr.connected += [dineRM, bd]
dineRM.connected += [kitchen, wr]
```

Whichever way you would like to model your environment is up to you.

Just keep in mind that you will eventually design the AI agent that will correspond to your model environment.

Your Turn

In Swift (or whichever programming language you want), create a code model of your home based on the to modelling directions above. First, do the "traffic light method" by creating a simple enumeration or array of the rooms in your house.

Then, as Object-Oriented Programming, model your home by having each room represented by Room instances. Then, connect each room accordingly.

Chapter 7: Your AI Knowledge & Abilities

==== ==== ==== ==== ====

Here, we go much more in-depth with an AI agent's knowledge and abilities.

You will have to determine how your AI agent will receive its information - including what abilities it can do.

There are two solutions to this: your AI agent either has all its knowledge given by default; or it will scout/observe/learn its environment and gain information this way. Also, you can choose a combination of both. For now, we focus on Default Knowledge and abilities.

AI Knowledge by Default

Your AI agent can receive, by default, a fixed set of all information it will ever need. If you believe some part of your AI agent's information won't change, you may model your AI agent's information this way.

For example, your AI agent may be a self-driving vehicle. The rules of the road will stay consistent in the long term. Also, its driving patterns and techniques will stay consistent too. The road maps will also stay consistent. Therefore, your self-driving vehicle can navigate its way through a city and make its way from two points.

EASIEST WAY TO LEARN SWIFT, Part 1

We've included a complementary guide to learning programming essentials and to help you become a better programmer.

As a way to help you understand it much more easily, we've set it up as simple as possible.

To easily run code, select an IDE (Integrated Development Environment: essentially somewhere that you write and run code) of your choice. For Mac computers, Xcode is a great choice for swift programming.You may also use online IDE's swiftstub.com or runswiftlang.com

======================== ======

1) The Basic Data Types.

Booleans:

These are essentially on-off switch values. In code, boolean values are going to be either TRUE or FALSE.

In Swift, booleans can only be in lower-case (i.e. true, false). Booleans cannot have any upper-case letters in them (i.e. TRUE, True)

Examples:

true, false

Strings:

These are sets of keyboard characters - including letters, numbers, and other symbols - arranged in some order to make a text phrase. They start and end with double quotation marks.

Examples:

" This is a String. "
" This 15 4 &^%$! 5tring too. "

Integers:

They're exactly as they're defined - whole numbers without any fractions or decimals. Here are some examples:

12
143
19999932

Floats: also called floating-point numbers, they represent the opposite of Integers - they are numbers beyond the decimal point. In Swift, you need to include at least one number before the decimal point - even 0 if you need to.

Example:

0.12 // a Float in Swift
.12 // NOT a Float in Swift

2a) Variables

Remember in grade school math where you used letters such as X and Y to represent numbers? Textbooks had phrases such as 'let x = 4' and 'let y = 19'. These were called variables.

Variables prevalently exist in programming too. But in programming, you can give your variables a name. And instead of numbers, variables can be whatever data you assign them as. They can be strings, booleans, integers, and more.

In Swift, you can create variables in the following syntax:

var (Variable Name) = (Initial Value);

Examples:

```
var a = " This is a String. "
var b = 122
var c = true
var d = 0.1234
```

Think of variables as one-sentence statements in the form of "(name) is a _____" . Use variables to tell the computer certain facts about your code. The concept is just as simple as telling me that a fire hydrant is red or the sky is blue.

2b) Constants

The Swift programming language also has Constants. They're much like variables, but the values never change.

In Swift, you can create constants in the following syntax:

let (Constant Name) = (Initial, unchanging Value);

Here are the same examples above, but as Constants:

```
let a = " This is a String. "
let b = 122
let c = true
let d = 0.1234
```

2c) Choosing between Variables and Constants

If you have to choose between Variables and Constants, think about what you plan to use them for.

If you have to modify or change the values, use Variables. If you absolutely don't, use Constants.

3) Composite Data

This concept means that a set of individual, lesser data are comprised together to form a whole, singular chunk of data. Put in the simplest way possible, if Variables are sentences, Composite Data are entire paragraphs that can be made of sentences.

The most commonly used composite data concept today are classes and structs. A class can be composed of any amount of variables and functions (we'll cover functions later).

In Swift, you can create classes in the following syntax:

```
class (Class Name) {
        // some code
}
```

Example:

```
class House {
        // insert code here
}
```

Swift also allows you to use Data Structures - referred to as 'Structs'.

In Swift, you can also create structs in the following syntax:

```
struct (Class Name) {
        // some code
}
```

Example:

```
struct House {
        // insert code here
}
```

NOTE: you'll encounter situations where you need to choose either classes or structs. The biggest difference is how they use '=' assignments:

Structs as values are COPIES.

Example:

```
var a = HouseStruct()        // <— A NEW STRUCT INSTANCE
var a2 = a                   // <— A -COPY- OF THAT NEW STRUCT INSTANCE
```

Classes as values can be REFERRED TO THE SAME CREATED DATA OBJECT.

Example:

```
var a = HouseClass() // <— A NEW CLASS INSTANCE
var a2 = a           // <— Referring to THAT SAME new Class Instance!
```

4a) Making Functions

If Variables are sentences, Functions are merely actions or verbs.

In essence, functions are outlined set of instructions. They are carried out by the computer once a line of code calls their names. For example, if a line of code told a computer to walk, the computer would follow the instructions to walk (i.e. one step forward, lean forward, step with other foot, etc.)

To create a function in Swift, follow this syntax:

```
func <Function Name>( input1: datatype1, ... ) ->
<output data type> {
// write code here
 // use the next line if the function outputs any data:
// return (variable name with data type, or any data)
}
```

If your function doesn't output anything, follow this syntax instead:

```
func <Function Name>( input1: datatype1, ... ) {
// write code here
}
```

4b) Setting up Data Types

In Swift, you'll have to define the data types you use in your functions. When doing this, use the proper syntax below for each data type:

Booleans: Use 'Bool'

Strings: Use 'String'

Integers: Use 'Int'

Floats: Use 'Float'

Here are some example functions in Swift:

```swift
func test1(a: String, b: Float) -> Bool {
   return true
}

func test2(a: Int, b: Bool) -> String {
   return "Okay"
}
```

```
func test3(a: Int, b: Bool) -> Void {
    // some code here
}
```

Furthermore, for classes and structs you define, you can just use their names when defining your functions' data types:

```
class Tree {
    // some code
}

func test4(t: Tree) {
    // some code
}
```

For now, it is HIGHLY recommended for you to use comments stating whether or not the function outputs anything. When you use the function, you can only call the function wherever its data output is expected.

Examples:

```
// returns an Integer, has no inputs:
func fXYZ() {
    // some code
        return 12
}
```

```
// doesn't return data, has 3 inputs:
func fABC(a: <some input>, b: <some input>, c: <some input>) {
    // some code
}
```

4c) Using Functions

To call a function, you just write its name, along with any inputs (if it needs them)

If the function doesn't output data (i.e. if it outputs void), follow this syntax - and make sure it's in its own line:

<Function Name>(any required inputs)

If the function DOES output some data, the syntax is similar as above. However, make sure the function is in a place where the output data type is expected:

var (variable name) = <Function Name>(any required inputs)

Examples:

// No Output:
func fABC(a: <some input>, b: <some input>, c: <some input>)

// Outputs an Integer:
var integer1 = func fXYZ()

EASIEST WAY TO LEARN SWIFT, Part 2

To easily run code, select an IDE (Integrated Development Environment: essentially somewhere that you write and run code) of your choice. For Mac computers, Xcode is a great choice for swift programming.You may also use online IDE's swiftstub.com or runswiftlang.com

================================ ======

Part 5a: Arrays in Swift

Arrays are a sequenced list of a certain data type. Those data types can be simple or compound data.

To set up an array, follow this syntax:

var (variable name) = [<data type>]()

Just like in Swift functions, you need to declare your data types for Swift arrays.

Example:

var a = [String]()

You can also access individual items based on that item's position within the array. 0 is the first item; the array size minus one is the last item.

(In programming, the very 1st number is often 0. Remember this!)

For example, you would get the first item of an array like so:

someArray[0]

And you would get the last item of an array like so:

// an Array with room for 10 items:
someArray[9]

Part 5b: Iteration

To process each item in an array, use these lines:

for x in (array name) {
        // every time you mention 'x' in this code,
        // it will be applied to every item within the array

}

For example, this would print out 1 to 5:

```
var a = [1,2,3,4,5]
for x in a {
        print(x)
}
```

Part 6: Logic & Operators

There are three Basic Logic Operators: AND, OR. and NOT.

AND and OR are used to compare two or more statements that are either True or False. They are used in the form of (x AND y) or (x OR y)

AND is true if all items between it is true. OR is true if either one of its items is true.

NOT returns the opposite of a single statement it's set to; so 'NOT true' would be false and 'NOT False' would be true.

In Swift, here are how the operators are:

AND operator: &&

OR operator: ||

NOT operator: !<boolean>

Examples:

```
// print false:
print (true && false)
// print true:
print (true || false)
// print false:
print (!true)
```

Part 7: IF-ELSE Statements

The concept is simple: There's a boolean statement to check. If it's true, do the procedure after the IF line. If it's false, do the procedure after the ELSE line.

```
if <insert something that would output a boolean> {
       // code that happens if true
}
else {
       // code that happens if false
}
```

Note that the conditional procedures are in between the curly brackets '{ }'.

an IF statement also doesn't need an ELSE statement; it can be by itself:

if <insert something that would output a boolean> {
*   // code that happens if true*
}

Examples:

// IF-ELSE together:
if age > 20 {
*   drinkingAge = true*
}
else {
*   drinkingAge = false*
}

// IF-statement alone:
if happy() and knowIt() {
*   hands.clap()*
}

EASIEST WAY TO LEARN OBJECT-ORIENTED

We've also included a complementary guide to learning Object-Oriented programming -one of the most popular types of programming in use today.

To easily run code, select an IDE (Integrated Development Environment: essentially somewhere that you write and run code) of your choice. For Mac computers, Xcode is a great choice for swift programming.You may also use online IDE's swiftstub.com or runswiftlang.com

========================= ======

1) Object Oriented Programming

In the world of programming, you will hear this term very very often.

This is because Object-Oriented Programming (OOP for short) is one of the most widely-used programming styles out there.

Do you remember the concept of "Classes" back in Part 1? You used this form of composite data to group up smaller data into a larger whole.

The main point of Object-Oriented Programming is this:

In object-oriented programming, you create 'copies' of those classes you've designed. In even simpler terms, A Class is a data structure that acts as "blueprints". Those "created copies" you've made, based on that class 'blueprints', are called Objects.

But why? Because as you learn more and more about programming, you will encounter the notion of Abstraction - applying a general idea across multiple times and scenarios - ultimately saving time, confusion, and effort.

Re-coding the same composite data over and over would lead to more effort and frustration, whereas re-using the same idea leads to efficiency and consistency.

2) OOP Terminology

Variables and Functions can take on new roles in OOP. They can be called Fields and Methods, respectively. In some cases, it's really up to you to use which names you want, just as long as you understand what other programmers mean when they use these terms.

Fields represent variables in OOP because, just like fields in any entry form, data objects can have fields with as many different values as you can think of.

Think of fields as a certain attribute for an object. Each object might have different attributes from each other:

```
class Cat{
        var color = "green"
}

// these cats are objects based on Cat class:
catA.color = "white"
catB.color = "grey"
catC.color = "orange"
```

Methods represent the functions that Objects have. Think of Methods as 'actions' and 'behaviours' that objects do.

In OOP, you can define a method within a class but you need to access the method from an object itself.

For example, if we create a few Cat objects based on some Cat Class, each Cat object would have all the methods defined on the Cat Class:

```
class Cat{
        func meow() {}
}

// these cats are objects based on Cat class:
catA.meow()
catB.meow()
catC.meow()
```

3) Constructor Methods

Constructors are special class methods. Based on the classes they belong to, they create Objects for you.

The constructor is simply your class name as a function. To create a data object based on a certain class, follow this syntax:

```
var c1 = Cat()
```

You're essentially setting some variable as a data object.

Example:

```
class House {
        // insert code here
}

let h = House()
```

To call a class object, simply refer to it:

Example:

```
let h = House()
var MyHouse = h
```

ARCHIVE A01: Frontier Search Algorithm

For the procedure below, select an IDE of your choice. If you have a mac computer, XCode will suffice. You may also use online IDE's such as swiftstub.com or runswiftlang.com

=========================== ======

This is the default Frontier Search Algorithm used by most chapters throughout the book.

It is strongly recommended to view this only after you've finished building & successfully testing the algorithm already.

```
class Node {
    var contents: String
    var children = [Node]()
    // CONSTRUCTOR:
    init(cont: String) {
        self.contents = cont
    }

}
```

```
/*
    // MAIN ALGORITHM: FRONTIER SEARCH
    */
    func search(query: String, n1: Node) -> Path {
        // - frontier:= {new array of Nodes}
        var frontier = [Path]()

        // - create a new Path and put the Start node in it
        let p = Path();
        p.contents.append(n1);

        // - put the new Path into the frontier
        frontier.append(p);

    while !frontier.isEmpty {
        // - select and remove a Path <s0, s1,....,sk> from
frontier;
        // (use helper function pickPath() )
        let pick = pickPath(&frontier);

        // If a node in the path has the goal, return
selected Path
        if hasGoal(query, p: pick) {
            return pick
            }

        else {
            // For every connected node of end node sk:
            let sk = pick.contents.last
            // - add copied Path <s0, s1,....,sk, s> to frontier;

            for i in sk!.children {
```

```
        // 1. Make a copy of the selected Path
        let toAdd = Path()


toAdd.contents.appendContentsOf(pick.contents)
        // - Add connected node of sk onto path copy
        toAdd.contents.append(i)
        // - add copied Path <s0, s1,....,sk, si> to
frontier;
        frontier.append(toAdd)
    }

  }

  }
  // (empty Path as output if no solution found)
  return Path()
}
```

```
/*
  // HELPER FUNCTION #1:
  // NOTE: you can modify the position assignment to
change the Search Strategy
  */
  func pickPath(inout f: [Path]) -> Path {
    let position = 0
    let ret = f[position]
    f.removeAtIndex(position)
    return ret;
  } ;

/*
  // HELPER FUNCTION #2:
  */
  func hasGoal(s: String, p: Path) -> Bool {

    for n in p.contents {
      if n.contents == s {return true}
    }
    return false;
  }
```

```
// The Path Class:
class Path {
    var contents = [Node]()
};
```

Printer Method:

Make sure to place this inside your code:

```
func printer(p: Path) -> String {
    if p.contents.isEmpty {return "NOTE: No Solution
Found";}
    else {
        var s = "Solution Found! Path: ";
        for i in p.contents {
            s += i.contents + ", "
        }
    return s;
    }
}
```

ARCHIVE A02: Bigger Search Graph

For DFS & BFS, Chapter SWIFT-03

For the procedure below, select an IDE of your choice. If you have a mac computer, XCode will suffice. You may also use online IDE's such as swiftstub.com or runswiftlang.com

=========================== ======

Reference Image:

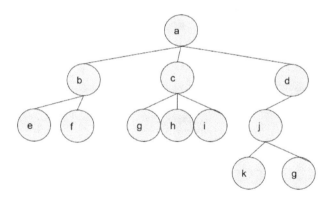

The code below is based on the default Node structure throughout the book.

```
var a = Node(cont: "a");
var b = Node(cont: "b");
var c = Node(cont: "c");
var d =  Node(cont: "d");
          var e = Node(cont: "e");
          var f = Node(cont: "f");
          var g1 = Node(cont: "g");
          var h = Node(cont: "h");
          var i = Node(cont: "i");
          var j = Node(cont: "j");
          var k = Node(cont: "k");
          var g2 = Node(cont: "g");
a.children.append(b);
a.children.append(c);
a.children.append(d);
b.children.append(e);
b.children.append(f);
c.children.append(g1);
c.children.append(h);
c.children.append(i);
d.children.append(j);
j.children.append(k);
j.children.append(g2);
```

ARCHIVE SWIFT-A3a: Solving Schedule Problems

AI to Solve Scheduling Problems

Using Generate-and-test Algorithm

Copy and paste the code below to an IDE of your choice:

```
var Anna = [9, 10, 11,12,13,14,15,16,17,18, 19, 20, 21, 22, 23]
var Betty = [9, 10, 11,12,13,14,15,16,17,18, 19, 20, 21, 22, 23]
var Cara = [9, 10, 11,12,13,14,15,16,17,18, 19, 20, 21, 22, 23]
var Donna = [9, 10, 11,12,13,14,15,16,17,18, 19, 20, 21, 22, 23]

// Goal 1: Have an hour of the day when EVERYONE is available to meet
// INPUT: Four Integers, representing Hours
// OUTPUT: Boolean
// EFFECT: return True if all input hours are equal
func g1(a: Int, b: Int, c: Int, d: Int)-> Bool{
    return (a == b && b == c && c == d)
}
```

```
// Constraint Functions
    // INPUT: an Integer, representing a friend's Hour
    // OUTPUT: Boolean
    // EFFECT: return True if the hour satisfies the time
constraints

// Constraint 1: Anna has classes 11am - 1:50pm
func c1(a: Int) -> Bool {
    return (a < 11 || a > 13)
}

// Constraint 2: Betty has classes noon - 3pm,
// then has dance practice until 4pm
func c2(b: Int) -> Bool {
    return (b < 12 || b >= 16)
}

// Constraint 3: Cara has work 7pm to 11pm
func c3(c: Int) -> Bool {
    return (c < 19 || c > 23)
}
```

```
// Constraint 4: Diana has volunteer hours from 6pm to
8pm,
// and work 8pm to 11pm
func c4(d: Int) -> Bool {
  return (d < 18 || d > 22)
}


// Main Algorithm: Generate and Search
for v in Anna {
  for w in Betty {
    for x in Cara {
      for y in Donna {
        if g1(v, b: w, c: x, d: y)
        && c1(v)
        && c2(w)
        && c3(x)
        && c4(y) {
          // === Solution Results are Here
          print("Anna, Betty, Cara, and Diana can
hang out at: "
          , v
          , ":00")
          //===
        }
      }
    } } }
```

ARCHIVE SWIFT-A3b: Solving Schedule Problems

AI to Solve Scheduling Problems

Using Generate-and-test Algorithm

Alternate Version: For Each Friend to schedule, Remove Unavailable Hours

Copy and paste the code below to an IDE of your choice:

```
var Anna = [9, 10, 11,12,13,14,15,16,17,18, 19, 20, 21, 22, 23]
var Betty = [9, 10, 11,12,13,14,15,16,17,18, 19, 20, 21, 22, 23]
var Cara = [9, 10, 11,12,13,14,15,16,17,18, 19, 20, 21, 22, 23]
var Donna = [9, 10, 11,12,13,14,15,16,17,18, 19, 20, 21, 22, 23]

// Goal 1: Have an hour of the day when EVERYONE is available to meet
// INPUT: Four Integers, representing Hours
// OUTPUT: Boolean
// EFFECT: return True if all input hours are equal
func g1(a: Int, b: Int, c: Int, d: Int)-> Bool{
    return (a == b && b == c && c == d)
}
```

```swift
// Constraint Procedures
// Constraint 1: Anna has classes 11am - 1:50pm
var delList = [Int]()
for a in Anna {
    if a >= 11 && a < 14 {
        delList.append(a)
    }
}
// (Delete ALL of Anna's unavailable hours)
for z in delList {
    var i = 0
    while i < Anna.count{
        if Anna[i] == z {
            Anna.removeAtIndex(i)
        }
        i++
    }

}
```

```
// Constraint 2: Betty has classes noon - 3pm,
// then has dance practice until 4pm
delList = []
for b in Betty {
  if b >= 12 && b < 16 {
    delList.append(b)
  }
}

// (Delete ALL of Betty's unavailable hours)
for z in delList {
    var i = 0
    while i < Betty.count{
      if Betty[i] == z {
        Betty.removeAtIndex(i)
      }
      i++
    }
}
```

```
// Constraint 3: Cara has work 7pm to 11pm
delList = []
for c in Cara {
   if c >= 19 && c <= 23 {
      delList.append(c)
   }
}
// (Delete ALL of Cara's unavailable hours)
for z in delList {
     var i = 0
     while i < Cara.count{
       if Cara[i] == z {
         Cara.removeAtIndex(i)
       }
       i++
     }
}

// Constraint 4: Donna has volunteer hours from 6pm to
8pm,
// and work 8pm to 11pm
delList = []
for d in Donna {
   if d >= 18 && d <= 22 {
      delList.append(d)   } }
```

```
// (Delete ALL of Donna's unavailable hours)
for z in delList {
    var i = 0
    while i < Donna.count{
      if Donna[i] == z {
        Donna.removeAtIndex(i)
      }
      i++
    }
}


// Main Algorithm: Generate and Search
for v in Anna {
  for w in Betty {
    for x in Cara {
      for y in Donna {
        if g1(v, b: w, c: x, d: y) {
          // === Solution Results are Here
          print("Anna, Betty, Cara, and Diana can
hang out at: "
            , v
            , ":00")
          //===
        }
      }   }   }   }
```

ARCHIVE SWIFT-A4a: Top Down Diagnosis

Top-Down Diagnosis of a Logic-Based System

Example code for the Water Flow System.

Note: In the code comments, you can find the original logic statements from the system.

Copy and paste the code below to an IDE of your choice.

Afterwards, call the Function topDownDiagnostic() and see what happens!

```
// ======= ====== ========
/*
// INPUTS:
// - a Boolean, for the Main Water Switch
// - a Boolean, for the Boiler Switch
// - three more Booleans, for each of taps D, E, and G
// OUTPUTS: none
// EFFECT: Run the Diagnostics to check if water can
flow through
// the washrooms, kitchen, and laundry washer
*/
```

```
var toiletConnected = true
var tapA = true
var tapB = true
var tapC = true
var tapF = true
var tapH = true

var toiletFlushable = true
var kitchenTap_Hot = true

func      topDownDiagnostic(mainwaterStatus:      Bool,
boilerStatus: Bool,
dStatus: Bool,
eStatus: Bool,
gStatus: Bool) {
    // A <- MainWaterSwitch
    if mainwaterStatus { tapA = true; }
    // B <- A
    if tapA { tapB = true;
       print( "Tap A is on. ") }
    // C <- B
    if tapB { tapC = true;
       print( "Tap B is on. ") }
```

```
// ToiletConnected <- D and C
if dStatus && tapC { toiletConnected = true;
    print( "Taps D and C are on. ") }


// ToiletFlushable <- ToiletConnected
if toiletConnected { toiletFlushable = true;
    print( "Toilet is Flushable.")
}
else {
    print( "Toilet Won't Flush.")
}


// F and H <- BoilerSwitch
if boilerStatus { tapF = true; tapH = true; }


// KitchenTap_Hot <- H
if tapH { kitchenTap_Hot = true;
    print( "Tap H is on.")
    print( "Hot water can flow through Kitchen Tap.") }

else {
    print( "There's no hot water from the Kitchen Tap.")
}
```

```
// KitchenTap_Cold <- E and C
if eStatus && tapC {
    print( "Cold water can flow through Kitchen Tap.") }

else {
    print( "There's no cold water from the Kitchen Tap.")
    }

// WashroomTap_Hot <- F and G
if gStatus && tapF {
    print( "Tap F is on.")
    print( "Hot water can flow through Washroom
Tap.")
}
else {
    print( "There's no hot water from the Washroom
Tap.")
    }

// WashroomTap_Cold <- C
if tapC {
    print( "Cold water can flow through Washroom
Tap.") }
else {
    print( "There's no cold water from the Washroom
Tap.")
    }
```

```
// LaundryWasher_Hot <- H
if tapH {
    print( "The Laundry washer has hot water.") }
else {
    print( "There's no hot water going into the Laundry
Washer.")
    }


// LaundryWasher_Cold <- E and C
if eStatus && tapC {
    print( "The Laundry washer has cold water.") }
else {
    print( "There's no cold water going into the Laundry
Washer.")
    }


// BathTubTap_Hot <- F
if tapF {
    print( "Hot water can flow through the Bath Tub
Tap.") }
else {
    print( "There's no hot water from the Bath Tub
Tap.")
    }


// BathTubTap_Cold <- B
if tapB {
    print( "Cold water can flow through the Bath Tub
Tap.") }
```

```
    else {
        print( "There's no cold water from the Bath Tub
Tap.")
        }
}
// ======= ====== ========


// Function call;
// Change the parameters to any Bool you want
topDownDiagnostic(true, boilerStatus: true,
dStatus: true,
eStatus: true,
gStatus: true)
```

ARCHIVE SWIFT-A4b: Bottom Up Diagnosis

Bottom-Up Diagnosis of a Logic-Based System

Example code for the Water Flow System.

Note: In the code comments, you can find the original logic statements from the system.

Copy and paste the code below to an IDE of your choice.

Afterwards, toggle any global variable between true/false, then call the Function BottomUpDiagnostic() and see what happens!

```
// ======= ====== ========
/*
// Global variables for independent switches/taps below.
// Switch them around between true/false,
// then run the Diagnostic on any water source.
*/
```

```
var mainWaterSwitch = true
var boilerSwitch = false
var tapD = true
var tapE = false
var tapG = true


var tapA = true
var tapB = true
var tapC = true
var tapF = true
var tapH = true
var toiletFlushable = true
var toiletConnected = true
var kitchenTap_Hot = true

/*
// INPUTS: Integers 1-5:
// This determines which water source in the house the
Diagnostic will check:
// 1: Toilet
// 2: Washroom Taps
// 3: Bath Tub Taps
// 4: Kitchen Taps
// 5: Washing Machine Water Feed
```

```
// OUTPUTS: none
// EFFECT: Run the Diagnostics to check if water can
feed to the
// Chosen water source in the house
*/
func botUpDiagnostic(mode: Int) {
   // A <- MainWaterSwitch
   if mainWaterSwitch { tapA = true
      print( "Main Water Switch is On.")
   }
   // B <- A
   if tapA { tapB = true
      print( "Tap A is on. ")
   }
   // C <- B
   if tapB {
      tapC = true
      print( "Tap B is on. ")
   }

   if mode == 1 {
```

```
      // ToiletConnected <- D and C
if tapD && tapC {
   toiletConnected = true;
   print( "Tap C is on. ");
   print( "Tap D is on. ");
}

// ToiletFlushable <- ToiletConnected
if toiletConnected {
   toiletFlushable = true;
   print( "Toilet is Flushable.")
   }
else {
   print( "Toilet Won't Flush.")
   }
   return
}

// F and H <- BoilerSwitch
if boilerSwitch {
   tapF = true;
   tapH = true;
   print( "Boiler Switch is On.") }
```

```
if mode == 2 {
    // WashroomTap_Hot <- F and G
    if tapG && tapF {
        print( "Tap F is on.")
        print( "Hot water can flow through Washroom Tap.")}
    else {
        print( "There's no hot water from the Washroom Tap.")
    }
    // WashroomTap_Cold <- C
    if tapC {
        print( "Tap C is on. ")
        print( "Cold water can flow through Washroom Tap.")
    }
    else {
        print( "There's no cold water from the Washroom Tap.")
    }
    return
}
```

```
if mode == 3 {
    // BathTubTap_Hot <- F
    if tapF {
        print( "Tap F is on.")
        print( "Hot water can flow through the Bath Tub Tap.")
    }
    else {
        print( "There's no hot water from the Bath Tub Tap.")
    }
    // BathTubTap_Cold <- B
    if tapB {
        print( "Cold water can flow through the Bath Tub Tap.")
    }
    else {
        print( "There's no cold water from the Bath Tub Tap.")
    }
    return
}
```

```
if mode == 4 {
  // KitchenTap_Hot <- H
  if tapH { kitchenTap_Hot = true;
    print( "Tap H is on.")
    print( "Hot water can flow through Kitchen Tap.")
  }
  else {
    print( "There's no hot water from the Kitchen Tap.")
    }
  // KitchenTap_Cold <- E and C
  if tapE && tapC {
    print( "Tap C is on.")
    print( "Tap E is on.")
    print( "Cold water can flow through Kitchen Tap.")
  }
  else {
    print( "There's no cold water from the Kitchen Tap.")
    }
    return
}
```

```
if mode == 5 {
    // LaundryWasher_Hot <- H
    if tapH {
        print( "Tap H is on.")
        print( "The Laundry washer has hot water.") }
    else {
        print( "There's no hot water going into the Laundry
Washer.")
        }
    // LaundryWasher_Cold <- E and C
    if tapE && tapC {
        print( "Tap C is on.")
        print( "Tap E is on.")
        print( "The Laundry washer has cold water.") }
    else {
        print( "There's no cold water going into the Laundry
Washer.")
        }
    return
        }

    }
// ======== ====== ========
```

```
// Function call;
// Change the mode to any integer 1-5
// Change the boolean variables around too
botUpDiagnostic(1)
```

www.ingramcontent.com/pod-product-compliance
Lightning Source LLC
LaVergne TN
LVHW022347060326
832902LV00022B/4294